ISAAC ASIMOV'S NEW LIBRARY OF THE UNIVERSE

STAR CYCLES:
THE LIFE AND DEATH OF STARS

BY ISAAC ASIMOV
WITH REVISIONS AND UPDATING BY FRANCIS REDDY

Gareth Stevens Publishing
MILWAUKEE

For a free color catalog describing Gareth Stevens' list of high-quality books, call 1-800-542-2595 (USA) or 1-800-461-9120 (Canada). Gareth Stevens' Fax: (414) 225-0377.

Library of Congress Cataloging-in-Publication Data

Asimov, Isaac.
  Star cycles: the life and death of stars / by Isaac Asimov; with
revisions and updating by Francis Reddy.
      p. cm. — (Isaac Asimov's New library of the universe)
  Rev. ed. of: The birth and death of stars. 1989.
  Includes index.
  ISBN 0-8368-1227-1
  1. Stars—Juvenile literature. I. Reddy, Frank, 1959-.
II. Asimov, Isaac. The birth and death of stars. III. Title.
IV. Series: Asimov, Isaac. New library of the universe.
QB801.7.A855   1995
523.8—dc20   95-7892

This edition first published in 1995 by
Gareth Stevens Publishing
1555 North RiverCenter Drive, Suite 201
Milwaukee, Wisconsin 53212, USA

Revised and updated edition © 1995 by Gareth Stevens, Inc. Original edition published in 1989 by Gareth Stevens, Inc. under the title *The Birth and Death of Stars*. Text © 1995 by Nightfall, Inc. End matter and revisions © 1995 by Gareth Stevens, Inc.

Series editor: Barbara J. Behm
Design adaptation: Helene Feider
Production director: Teresa Mahsem
Editorial assistant: Diane Laska
Picture research: Matthew Groshek and Diane Laska

Printed in the United States of America

1 2 3 4 5 6 7 8 9 99 98 97 96 95

To bring this classic of young people's information up to date, the editors at Gareth Stevens Publishing have selected two noted science authors, Greg Walz-Chojnacki and Francis Reddy. Walz-Chojnacki and Reddy coauthored the recent book *Celestial Delights: The Best Astronomical Events Through 2001*.

Walz-Chojnacki is also the author of the book *Comet: The Story Behind Halley's Comet* and various articles about the space program. He was an editor of *Odyssey*, an astronomy and space technology magazine for young people, for eleven years.

Reddy is the author of nine books, including *Halley's Comet, Children's Atlas of the Universe, Children's Atlas of Earth Through Time*, and *Children's Atlas of Native Americans*, plus numerous articles. He was an editor of *Astronomy* magazine for several years.

CONTENTS

We live in an enormously large place – the Universe. It's just in the last fifty-five years or so that we've found out how large it probably is. It's only natural that we would want to understand the place in which we live, so scientists have developed instruments – such as radio telescopes, satellites, probes, and many more – that have told us far more about the Universe than could possibly be imagined.

We have seen planets up close. We have learned about quasars and pulsars, black holes, and supernovas. We have gathered amazing data about how the Universe may have come into being and how it may end. Nothing could be more astonishing.

We have also come to understand that the Universe changes. It may not seem to be changing because the events can happen so slowly. For instance, stars come into being, change with time, and grow older. But all this happens over a great deal of time. Eventually, the stars come to an end, sometimes in violent ways.

Isaac Asimov

A Star Is Born

Stars are born within giant gas clouds. Gas and dust swirl deep in these clouds. This action forms pockets of gas. Deep in one cloud, a pocket of gas grows large enough that its gravity pulls more gas into it. Gradually, its center begins to contract, and it warms up.

The pocket of gas spins slowly at first, but then it spins ever faster. The swirling gas flattens into a disk. Eventually, its hot central part begins to produce energy on its own – and a star is born. It may remain hidden within the cloud for millions of years, but it will emerge. Perhaps planets will form before the young star's energy blows the surrounding disk away.

In another part of the same great dark gas cloud, an older star has reached the end of its ability to produce energy. It suddenly collapses and then explodes, returning its material to the cloud from which it was born. The powerful blast stirs up the gas and creates new pockets – and perhaps new stars.

Right: Out of this cool, dark gas cloud somewhere in the Galaxy, a star has begun to form out of a clump of gas.

Opposite: The young star grows as its gravity gathers more gas from the surrounding cloud.

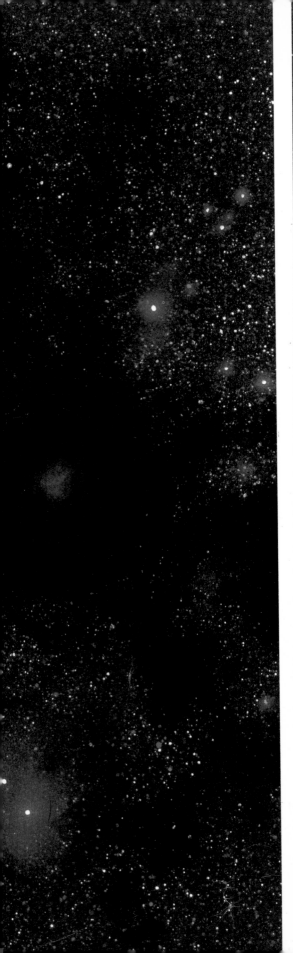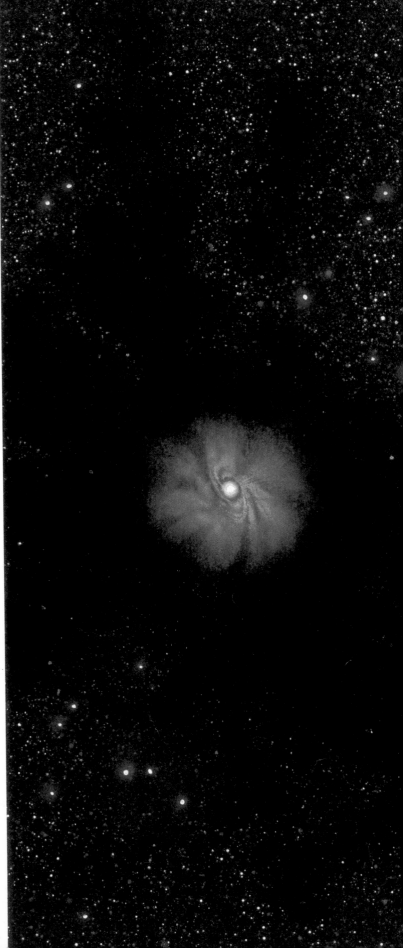

A Stellar Nursery

The Orion Nebula is one of the closest regions of recent star formations. It is about 1,500 light-years away from Earth. Hot, young stars at its center supply the energy that makes its gas glow.

The Orion Nebula itself is only a small part of a cloud that spans an entire constellation. Dust in the cloud blocks the light of the young stars within it, but the dust is warmed by those stars. Instruments sensitive to heat can detect the warmth. The colorful Orion Nebula is really just a bubble of gas blown off of this great invisible gas cloud. The stars that make the Orion Nebula shine have only just broken out of their nursery.

Opposite: A cluster of hot, young stars in the center of the Orion Nebula causes its gas to glow.

Inset: The Infrared Astronomical Satellite made this map of the vast Orion Molecular Cloud. The brightest areas are the hottest. The bright area just below the center of the image is the Orion Nebula.

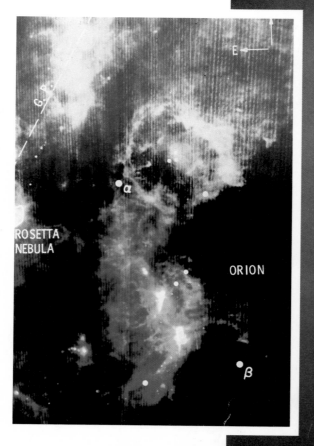

Inside the Orion Nebula

A cluster of young, very bright stars has formed near the edge of the star-forming region in the Orion Nebula. These stars, called the Trapezium, are hotter and brighter than our Sun. They are so hot that most of the energy they give off is ultraviolet radiation, not visible light.

This ultraviolet radiation has a great effect on the nebula. It causes the gas surrounding the stars to glow green, blue, red, and yellow up to a distance of five light-years away. Great shock waves ripple outward from the Trapezium as gas heated by the stars collides with cooler gas. These waves create the delicate wisps and filaments we see in the nebula.

At least half of the young stars are surrounded by dusty disks of material. How many planets might there be in the Orion Nebula?

! Multiple stars – not as odd as you might think!

Often a cloud of gas will collapse – not into a star, but into two or more closely spaced stars. When such multiple stars were first discovered, they were thought to be rare. Now scientists think that at least half of all stars are multiple. What makes a cloud condense into a single star or into multiple stars, and how does that influence the formation of planets? Scientists do not yet know.

Right: This image from the Very Large Array radio telescope reveals a web of stringlike filaments in the center of the Orion Nebula around hot Trapezium stars.

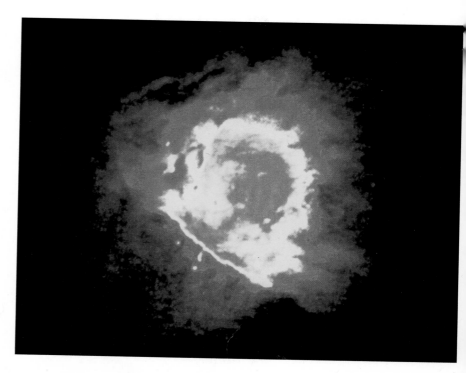

Above: The Hubble Space Telescope captured this image of the Orion Nebula. The picture shows an area just over one light-year across. The small blobs in the center are stars surrounded by disks of matter twice the diameter of our Solar System.

Our Average Sun

Stars come in all sizes. Our Sun is about average in size. Once a star forms, the heat it produces by nuclear fusion expands it enough to offset its gravitational pull. The star remains stable and doesn't change very much for millions of years.

Our Sun has been shining for about 4.5 billion years and is only middle-aged. It will keep shining as it is for about 5 billion more years. The hydrogen at its center changes slowly to helium, and the heat produced gives us light and warmth and makes it possible for life to exist on Earth.

Opposite, top: Many stars have partners. The Sun, the star on which life on Earth depends, is a single star.

Opposite, bottom: Scientists actually know very little about our Sun. For instance, they cannot explain what causes the Sun's dark, cooler areas known as sunspots *(pictured, upper right).*

The Brilliance of the Stars

Most stars are both smaller and cooler than the Sun, shining with a dim red light. A few are larger, hotter, and more luminous than our Sun. The two brightest stars located in the constellation known as the Southern Cross are thousands of times more luminous than our Sun. The star Beta Centauri is over 8,200 times as luminous, and the star Rigel is over 52,000 times as luminous as our Sun.

To remain so bright, very large stars must use their hydrogen quickly. Even though their large sizes give them a huge supply, such stars do not last as long as others. They shine for only a few million years before using up their hydrogen.

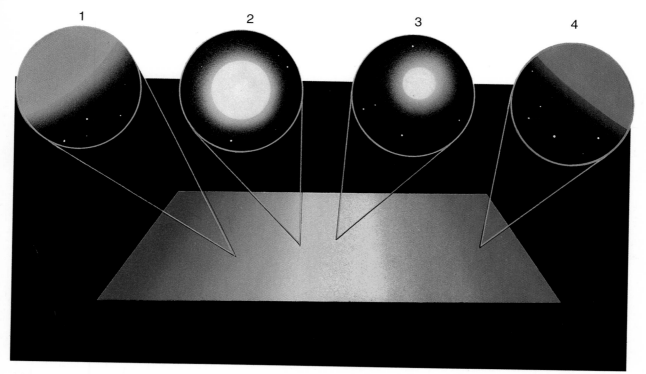

Above: The color of light a star produces depends on its mass, age, and temperature. Hot, young, and massive blue-white stars like Lambda Cephei (1) and Sirius (2) burn their fuel quickly. A massive star near the end of its life, like Betelgeuse (4), glows a cooler red but gives off great heat because of its large surface. As a relatively small, cool star, our yellow Sun (3) burns its fuel much more slowly.

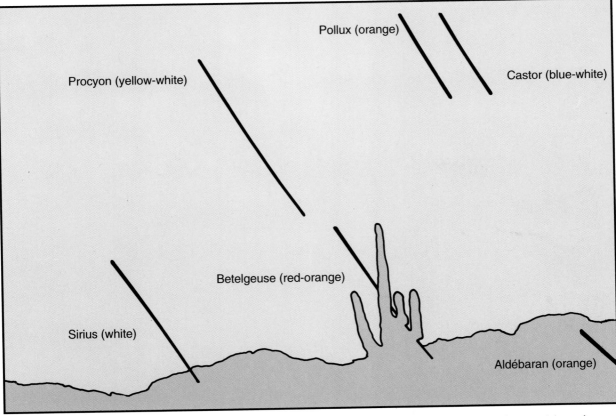

Pollux (orange)

Procyon (yellow-white)

Castor (blue-white)

Betelgeuse (red-orange)

Sirius (white)

Aldébaran (orange)

Top and bottom: Different types of stars have different colors caused by different stellar temperatures. Star trails *(upper, identified in the lower diagram)* display a range of pale, barely detectable colors. The brightest nighttime star is Sirius.

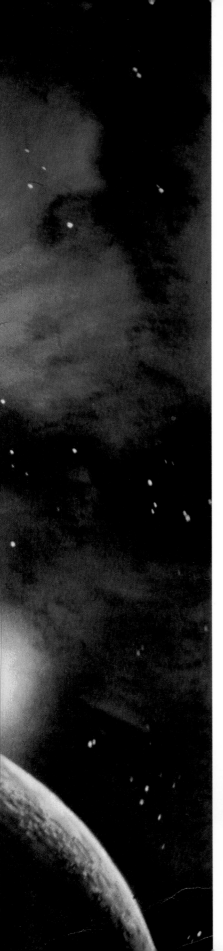

Giants of the Sky

When a star shines steadily, it is on what is known as its "main sequence." Our Sun is in its main sequence now.

Eventually, a star collects more and more helium in its center. As its hydrogen fuel runs out, the star contracts and squeezes its helium. The central temperature rises until the helium atoms begin to form still more complicated atoms – carbon, oxygen, and even heavier elements like iron. The extra heat makes the outer layers of the star expand; the star grows larger and larger. As the outer layers expand, they become cooler and glow red hot. Such stars are called red giants. All stars become red giants as their hydrogen runs low, but large ones become supergiants.

Betelgeuse, which is in Orion, is a red giant that might be as much as 700 million miles (1.13 billion km) across. That's more than 800 times as wide as our Sun!

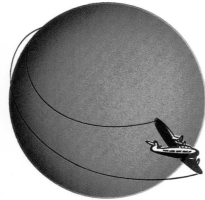

Left: Flying at about 200 miles (320 km) an hour, an old-fashioned plane like the one shown here would need about 1.5 years to fly around our "small" Sun. But flying around a red giant like Betelgeuse would take over 800 times as long or about 1,200 years.

Far left: An artist imagines a planetary system near a red giant. In a few billion years, our Sun will become a red giant.

Supernova – Star Bright

When enough atoms of iron and other heavy elements build up in a star's center, the star can no longer produce energy. Without the fierce heat of its central core, the star cannot balance its own gravity. It collapses suddenly, which creates an explosion that releases tremendous amounts of energy. The star is blown apart!

Scientists believe that only very large stars – or small stars that attract matter from a nearby companion star – can explode into what is called a supernova. During the explosion, the star's outer layers grow so hot that, for a few weeks, a single supernova will shine as brightly as an entire galaxy of stars.

Opposite: Pictured is the Crab Nebula, a remnant of a star that exploded as a supernova in the year 1054. The explosion could be seen in daylight for weeks.

Inset: Over five light-years across, the supernova remnant known as Cassiopeia A emits radio waves as it expands into space. This image was made using the Very Large Array radio telescope in New Mexico.

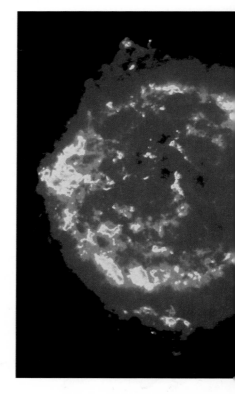

? *Can supernovas be predicted?*

Supernovas always catch us by surprise. They're usually well under way before they are seen. If scientists could predict when a star might explode, instruments could be put in place to study the first moments of the explosion and even the time before it. But scientists cannot yet predict supernovas. They know a star has to be in the red giant stage, but whether a particular red giant will explode tomorrow or ten thousand years from now is a puzzle.

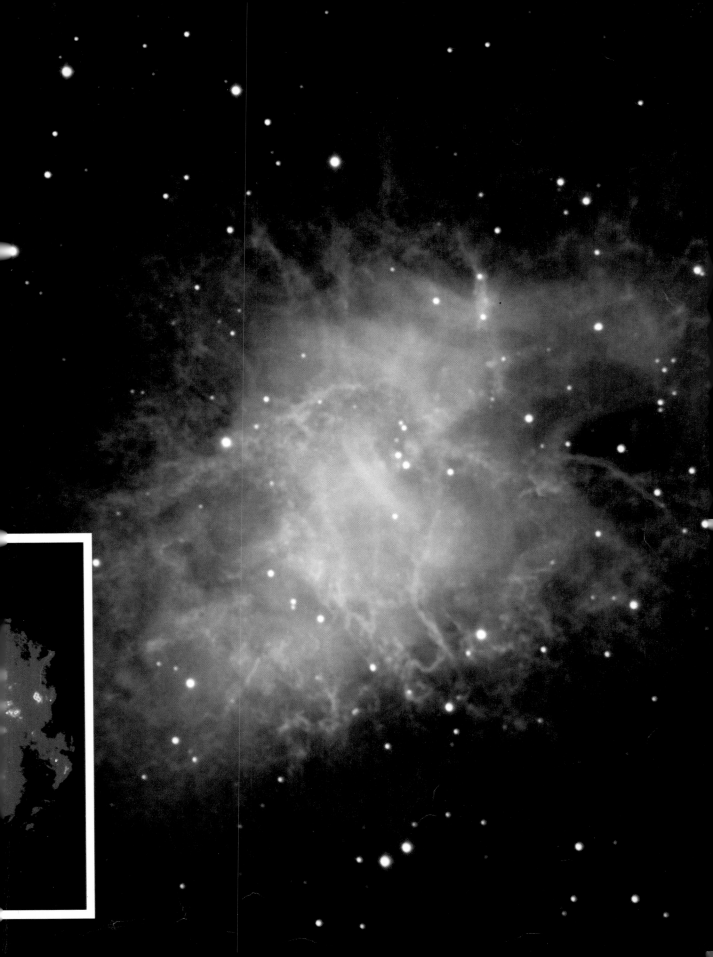

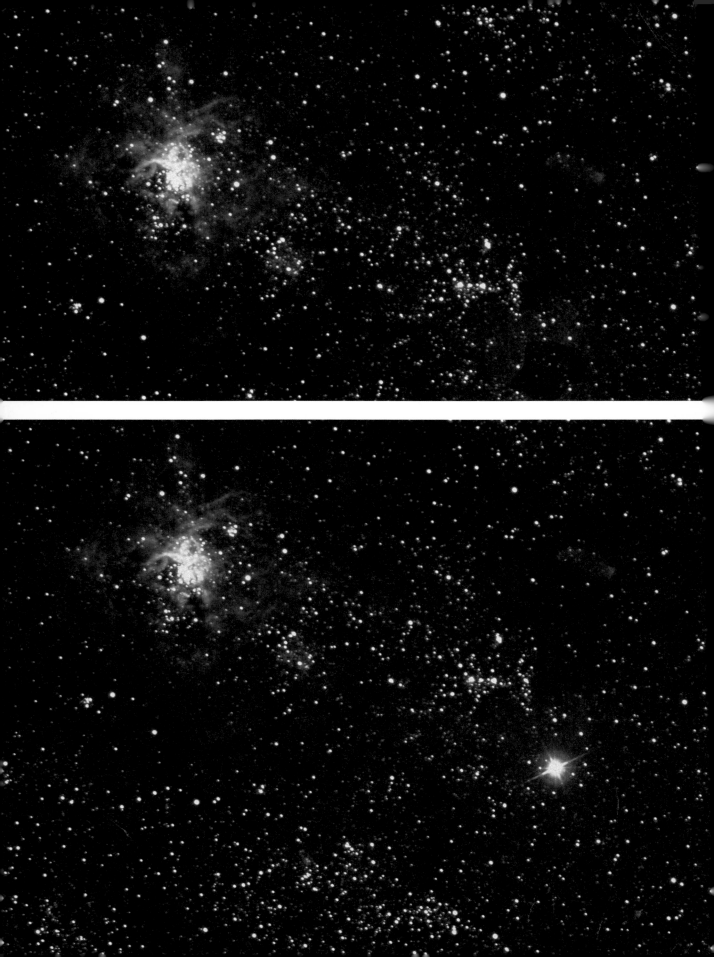

A Supernova for Our Times

Below: The Hubble Space Telescope revealed the bright expanding ring from Supernova 1987A. This image, taken in 1994, also revealed two additional rings. Astronomers are not sure how to explain this supernova's "three-ring circus."

Opposite: The latest known supernova appeared to astronomers in 1987. The area before the explosion is *at top*. The *bottom* photo was taken just after the explosion. The bright new star is not new at all. It is the final burst of light from a large and unstable star.

Since 1604, scientists have studied supernovas that have occurred in far distant galaxies and that could only be dimly seen through telescopes. But in February 1987, a supernova exploded in the Large Magellanic Cloud, a small galaxy only about 160,000 light-years from Earth. This was the closest supernova to our planet in nearly four centuries. It was a billion times as bright as our Sun! This supernova was named Supernova 1987A.

For the first time, advanced instruments could be used to study a supernova. Scientists were able to study just how radiation and particles called neutrinos were given off and how a cloud of gas formed and expanded.

! A look back in time

Although we saw a star explode in February 1987, that is not when it exploded. The supernova is 160,000 light-years from us. That means light from it takes 160,000 years to reach us. The explosion took place some 160,000 years ago, but the light from it just reached Earth in 1987. Some very distant objects are about 17 billion light-years away. We see them as they looked 17 billion years ago. That's how long it took their light to reach us.

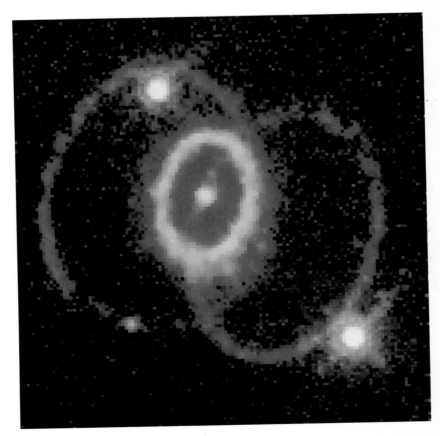

Transforming the Giants

As a star like our Sun collapses, gravity breaks its atoms into smaller pieces and forces them close together. The whole mass of a star can be squeezed into an object about the size of Earth. This shrunken star shines white hot and is called a white dwarf.

A still larger star collapses more violently, squeezing the pieces of atoms. For instance, after a supernova explosion dies down, what was once a red giant becomes a tiny, tightly packed ball perhaps only 8 miles (13 km) across. This is a neutron star.

Squeezed even more tightly together, the center of a collapsing star could become a black hole.

! *Neutron stars – fast and deadly*

Neutron stars spin very rapidly, often many times a second. Recently, astronomers have found some neutron stars that rotate over six hundred times each second. They have also found neutron stars that circle ordinary stars. With their powerful gravitational pull, the neutron stars slowly draw the material out of the ordinary stars into themselves, destroying the stars.

Opposite: A star exploded long ago, leaving behind a dense neutron star. Its companion, now an aged red giant, loses part of its atmosphere to the intense gravity of the neutron star. This fresh gas will let the neutron star shine again.

Above: Weighing a scant 0.00002 pound (0.000009 kg), a cup of average red giant matter (1) would barely lower a scale. A cup of matter from a star like our Sun (2) would weigh 0.73 pound (0.333 kg). The scale would crumble under a 5.1-million-pound (2.3-million-kg) cup of white dwarf matter (3). And a cup of neutron star matter (4) would register an amazing 730 trillion pounds (331 trillion kg) – if you could find a scale to weigh it on!

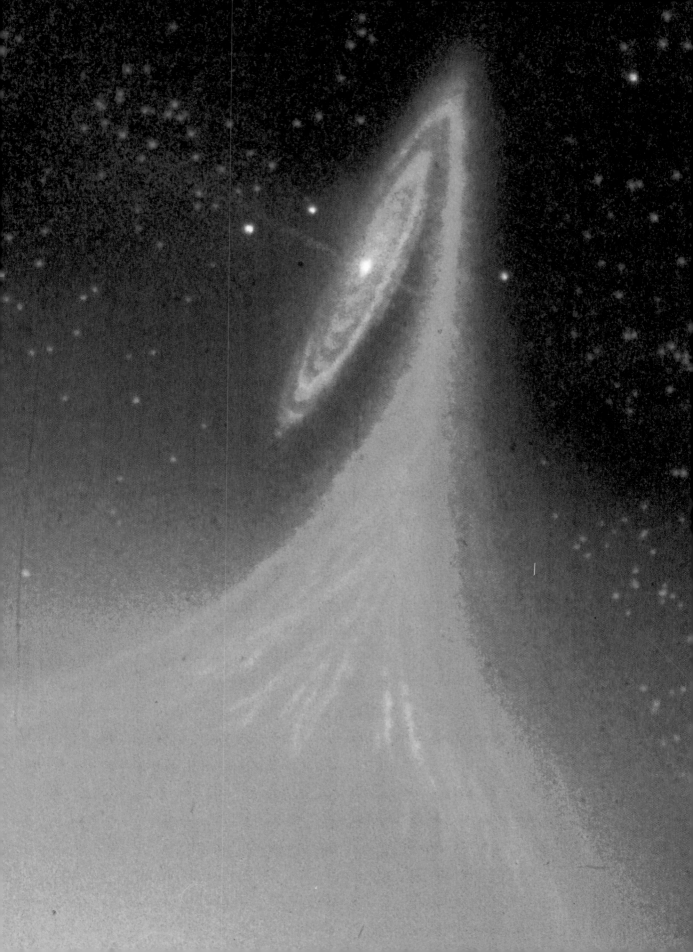

Earth's End

Someday our Sun will die, too, or at least it will cease being the kind of star it is now. About five billion years from now, it will start consuming helium in its core. It will start expanding and turning red. The Sun's surface will be cooler than it is now. But as it expands, there will be so much surface that the total amount of heat will become far greater than it is now.

Due to the Sun's increased heat, life on Earth will become impossible. Eventually, in fact, the Sun will expand so much that it will swallow Mercury, Venus, and Earth. In time, it will engulf even Mars. By that time, Earth will have turned into vapor. Our planet will no longer exist.

Life on Earth developed as our Sun settled into its current stage *(bottom, left)*. In a few billion years, when the Sun expands into a red giant, things will change quite a bit. First, the ocean water will turn into vapor, creating thick clouds *(bottom, center)*. In time, Earth's oceans will boil away. Our planet's crust will soften and begin to melt *(bottom, right)*. Before Earth becomes lost in the growing outer layers of the Sun, our neighboring Moon will dissolve *(top)*.

The Final Days of Our Sun

Although Earth will be gone, the Sun will still exist for a time as a red giant. Less than a billion years after it becomes a red giant, the Sun will collapse. It will be too small to collapse violently enough to become a supernova. It will become a white dwarf, scattering its outermost layers in all directions and forming a shell of gas called a planetary nebula. There are some of these already in the sky – white dwarfs shining within a shell of expanding gas.

The Sun will continue to shine as a white dwarf for billions of years, until, like a burned-up cinder, it will gradually cool into a black dwarf.

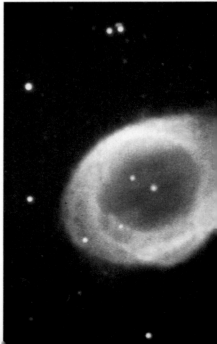

Ring nebulas are gaseous shells lit up by white dwarfs, the final remains of Sunlike stars. Because of their disk-like appearance in telescopes, these clouds are called planetary nebulas. Pictured is a gallery of planetary nebulas.

Top: A red giant as seen from a planet at a "safe" distance. Groups of sunspots dot its ruddy surface, and giant flares loop gas filaments far into space.

Bottom, left: The Ring Nebula in the constellation Lyra.

Bottom, center: The Bug Nebula in Scorpius.

Bottom, right: The Eskimo Nebula in Gemini.

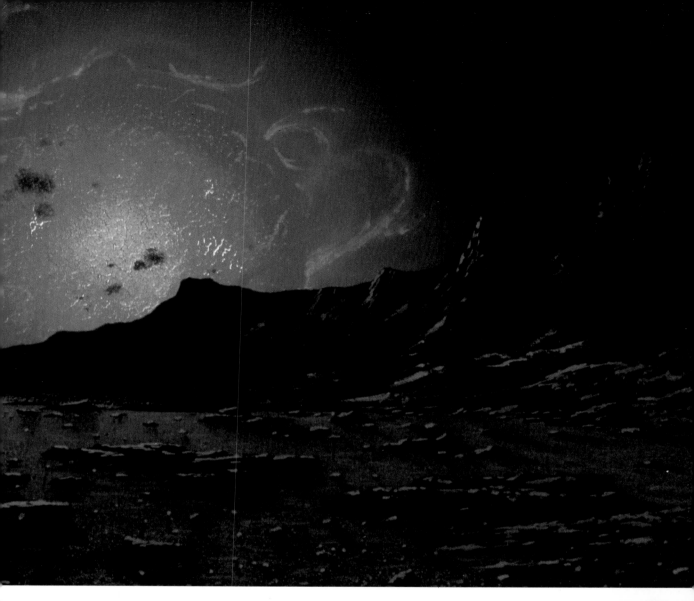
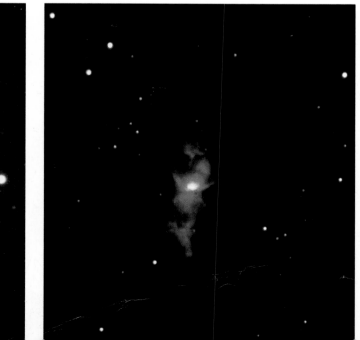
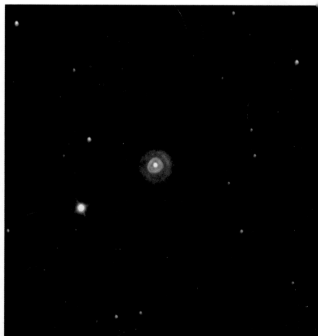

Born of the Stars

Out of the deaths of stars may come the births of other stars. When a supernova explodes, most of its matter is scattered through space. This matter contains atoms more complicated than those of hydrogen and helium, such as carbon, oxygen, silicon, and iron. The clouds of gas that still exist between the stars start to contain these complicated atoms. New stars form out of these clouds, and they too contain the complicated atoms.

Because these stars are "born" out of matter from earlier stars, they are called second-generation stars. Our Sun is an example of a second-generation star. Earlier stars could only have planets made up of hydrogen and helium, somewhat like Jupiter. Only second-generation stars can have planets made of rock and metal, like Earth.

And since the complicated atoms that make up our bodies also had their origins in ancient stellar matter, we, too, are "born" of the stars!

❗ Children of the stars

After the Big Bang, only hydrogen and helium atoms formed. Atoms more complex than these formed later in the centers of stars. These atoms were then spread throughout space by giant supernova explosions. Our planet Earth and most of our own bodies are made up almost entirely of these complex atoms. Almost every atom within our planet and ourselves was formed at the center of some star that once exploded violently. We are children of the stars.

Left: The next time you take a stroll beneath the Milky Way, imagine the stars as your cosmic birthplace.

Fact File: Starlight

All stars are born approximately the same way. But their sizes and masses affect how long they live – and how they die. The smallest stars are only about 8 miles (13 km) across, while the largest ones are millions of times bigger than our Sun. Use the chart on these two pages to follow the lives of three "typical" stars – a giant star, a star about the size and mass of our Sun, and a star about a third the mass of our Sun.

Time from Nebula Stage	Giant Star (15 solar masses)	Average Star (1 solar mass)	Small Star (1/3 solar mass)
10,000 years	Matter contracts into large ball. Resulting giant star has a lot of matter but burns very quickly.		
1 million years		Matter contracts into hot core; protostar forms – about 20 times Sun's brightness and width.	
10-11.6 million years	Helium created by nuclear fusion begins to build up in core. As the star feeds on its helium, it expands to as much as 100 times the diameter of our Sun.		Temperature inside the core of the nebula that will give birth to a red dwarf is just high enough to start burning. Low temperature means future red dwarf star will burn its hydrogen slowly and "live" longer than larger stars.
11.9 million years	The star expands into a red supergiant. As the massive star continues to burn, its outer layers explode into a supernova! At the center of the explosion, a tiny – perhaps only 8 miles (13 km) wide – but incredibly massive neutron star is left.		

After a "short" life of a few million years, the 15-solar-mass giant star has burned itself out. But the other two stars have barely begun their lives.

Time from Nebula Stage	Average Star (1 solar mass)	Small Star (1/3 solar mass)
70 million years	Hydrogen atoms in protostar begin the fusion process. Protostar becomes a star.	
1 billion years		Red dwarf now fully formed. Average surface temperature might reach only about 4,900°F (2,700°C) – cool for a star.
4.5 billion years	The star is now just like our Sun.	
7-9 billion years	Star begins to run out of hydrogen. As it burns remaining hydrogen, its temperature and size increase.	
10-11 billion years	Star begins to consume its helium and balloons into a red giant. By now, any planets once suitable for life – like Earth – have long been turned into lifeless wastelands. At its largest, this star is 400 times the diameter of our Sun – big enough to swallow Mars in its orbit!	The giant star has been "dead" for about 10 billion years. The star like our Sun is starting to explode into a red giant. But the red dwarf – slow, steady, and stable – is still just starting its life.
11-11.7 billion years	As star uses up its fuel, it shrinks into a white dwarf only about as big as Earth.	
50-100 billion years	As far as we know, the Universe is only 17-20 billion years old. But we think that the white dwarf may burn out completely in 50 billion years – and become a black dwarf.	Red dwarf stars may burn on quietly for some 100 billion years. They might become tiny white dwarfs or even brown dwarfs. No one knows for certain.

More Books about Stars

All About Stars. Jefferies (Troll)
The Birth of Our Universe. Asimov (Gareth Stevens)
Bright Stars, Red Giants and White Dwarfs. Berger (Putnam)
Mysteries of Deep Space: Black Holes, Pulsars, and Quasars. Asimov (Gareth Stevens)
Our Planetary System. Asimov (Gareth Stevens)
A Stargazer's Guide. Asimov (Gareth Stevens)
The Stars: From Birth to Black Hole. Darling (Dillon)
Stars and Galaxies. Apfel (Franklin Watts)
The Sun and Its Secrets. Asimov (Gareth Stevens)
Sun and Stars. Barrett (Franklin Watts)

Videos

Astronomy 101: A Beginner's Guide to the Night Sky. (Mazon)
The Birth and Death of Stars. (Gareth Stevens)
The Sun. (Gareth Stevens)

Places to Visit

You can explore the remote reaches of the Galaxy and discover the wonders of the stars without leaving Earth. Here are some museums and centers where you can find a variety of space exhibits.

NASA Lyndon B. Johnson Space Center
2101 NASA Road One
Houston, TX 77058

National Air and Space Museum-Smithsonian
Seventh and Independence Avenue, SW
Washington, D.C. 20560

Australian Museum
6-8 College Street
Sydney, NSW 2000 Australia

Edmonton Space and Science Centre
11211 - 142nd Street
Edmonton, Alberta T5M 4A1

San Diego Aero-Space Museum
2001 Pan American Plaza - Balboa Park
San Diego, CA 92101

The Space and Rocket Center and Space Camp
One Tranquility Base
Huntsville, AL 35807

Places to Write

Here are some places you can write for more information about the stars. Be sure to state what kind of information you would like. Include your full name and address.

National Space Society
922 Pennsylvania Avenue SE
Washington, D.C. 20003

The Planetary Society
65 North Catalina
Pasadena, CA 91106

Canadian Space Agency
Communications Department
6767 Route de L'Aeroport
Saint Hubert, Quebec J3Y 8Y9

Sydney Observatory
P. O. Box K346
Haymarket 2000 Australia

Glossary

the Big Bang: a gigantic explosion that some scientists believe created our Universe.

billion: the number represented by 1 followed by nine zeroes – 1,000,000,000. In some countries, this number is called "a thousand million." In these countries, one billion would then be represented by 1 followed by twelve zeroes – 1,000,000,000,000 – a million million.

black dwarf star: a "dead" star. When a star like our Sun uses up its store of hydrogen energy and collapses, it becomes a shining white dwarf star. When a white dwarf stops giving off light, it becomes a black dwarf.

black hole: a massive object – usually a collapsed star – so tightly packed that not even light can escape the force of its gravity.

galaxy: any of the many large groupings of stars, gas, and dust that exist in the Universe.

helium: a light, colorless gas that makes up part of every star.

hydrogen: a colorless, odorless gas that is the simplest and lightest of the elements. Most stars are three-quarters hydrogen.

luminous: producing light.

main sequence: a class of stars that shows a stable relationship between brightness, size, and temperature; the "middle age" of a star's life – the age into which our Sun falls.

nebula: a cloud of dust and gas in space. Some large nebulas, or nebulae, are the birthplaces of stars. Other nebulae are the debris of dying stars.

neutrino: extremely tiny particles produced when hydrogen fuses to helium in the center of a star.

neutron star: a star with all the mass of an ordinary large star but with its mass squeezed into a much smaller ball.

nuclear fusion: the smashing together of highly heated hydrogen atoms. This fusion of atoms creates helium and produces tremendous amounts of energy.

planetary nebula: a shell of gas expelled by a red giant star that has used up much of its hydrogen fuel, leaving the star's core as a brightly shining white dwarf.

proto-: the earliest or first form of something. In this book, a young star is a "protostar."

radiation: the spreading of heat, light, or other forms of energy by rays or waves.

radio waves: electromagnetic waves that can be detected by radio receiving equipment.

red dwarf star: a cool, faint star, smaller than our Sun. Red dwarfs are probably the most numerous stars in our Galaxy, but they are so faint that they are extremely difficult to see.

red giant: a huge star that develops when its hydrogen runs low and the extra heat makes it expand. Its outer layers then change to a cooler red.

supernova: a star that has collapsed, heating its cool outer layers and causing a huge explosion.

white dwarf: the small, white-hot body that remains when a star uses up its store of nuclear energy and collapses but does not explode.

Index

Born in 1920, Isaac Asimov came to the United States as a young boy from his native Russia. As a young man, he was a student of biochemistry. In time, he became one of the most productive writers the world has ever known. His books cover a spectrum of topics, including science, history, language theory, fantasy, and science fiction. His brilliant imagination gained him the respect and admiration of adults and children alike. Sadly, Isaac Asimov died shortly after the publication of the first edition of *Isaac Asimov's Library of the Universe.*

The publishers wish to thank the following for permission to reproduce copyright material: front cover, © Rick Sternbach; 4-5, 5, © Paul Dimare 1988; 6, Jet Propulsion Laboratory; 6-7, NOAO; 8, Courtesy of NRAO/AUI; 9, C. R. O'Dell/Rice University/NASA; 11 (upper), © Matthew Groshek 1980; 11 (lower), NOAO; 12, © Brian Sullivan 1989; 13 (upper), © Allan Morton; 13 (lower), Sharon Burris/© Gareth Stevens, Inc.; 14-15, © Paul Dimare; 15, Kate Kriege/© Gareth Stevens, Inc.; 16-17, Courtesy of NRAO/AUI; 17, © 1993 by Richard Wainscoat and John Kormendy, Institute for Astronomy, University of Hawaii; 18 (both), NOAO; 19, Dr. Christopher Burrows, ESA/STScI and NASA; 20, © Lynette Cook 1988; 21, © Paul Dimare 1988; 22-23 (all), 24-25 (upper), © John Foster; 24-25 (lower), 25 (left), NOAO; 25 (right), © 1984/University of Hawaii Institute of Astronomy, by Jack Marling and Wayne Annala, 24" f/15 telescope; 26-27, © Greg Mort 1987.